HAL•LEONARD

JAZZ PLAY-ALONG

Book and CD for B♭, E♭, C and Bass Clef Instruments

volume 144

Arranged and Produced by
Mark Taylor and Jim Roberts

Lee morgan

BOOK

CD

ISBN 978-1-4584-1645-2

HAL•LEONARD® CORPORATION

7777 W. Bluemound Rd. P.O. Box 13819 Milwaukee, WI 53213

Visit Hal Leonard Online at
www.halleonard.com

T0050717

LEE MORGAN

Volume 144

Arranged and Produced by
Mark Taylor and Jim Roberts

Featured Players:

Graham Breedlove–Trumpet
John Desalme–Tenor Sax
Tony Nalker–Piano
Regan Brough–Bass
Todd Harrison–Drums

**Recorded at Bias Studios, Springfield, Virginia
Bob Dawson, Engineer**

HOW TO USE THE CD:

Each song has <u>two</u> tracks:

1) Split Track/Melody

Woodwind, Brass, Keyboard, and **Mallet Players** can use
this track as a learning tool for melody style and inflection.

Bass Players can learn and perform with this track –
remove the recorded bass track by turning down the
volume on the LEFT channel.

Keyboard and **Guitar Players** can learn and perform with
this track – remove the recorded piano part by turning down
the volume on the RIGHT channel.

2) Full Stereo Track

Soloists or **Groups** can learn and perform with this
accompaniment track with the RHYTHM SECTION only.

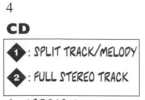

CEORA

BY LEE MORGAN

C VERSION

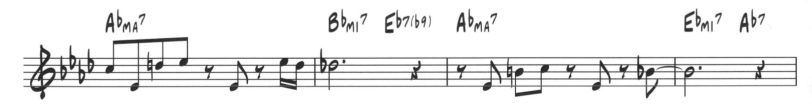

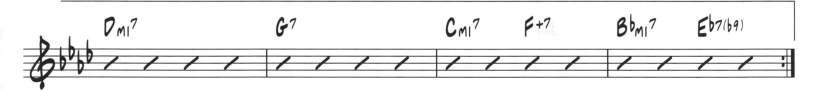

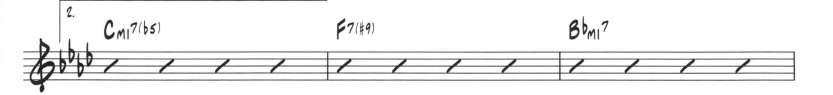

CD
◆ 3 : SPLIT TRACK/MELODY
◆ 4 : FULL STEREO TRACK

C VERSION

CORN BREAD

BY LEE MORGAN

MEDIUM 60'S FUNK

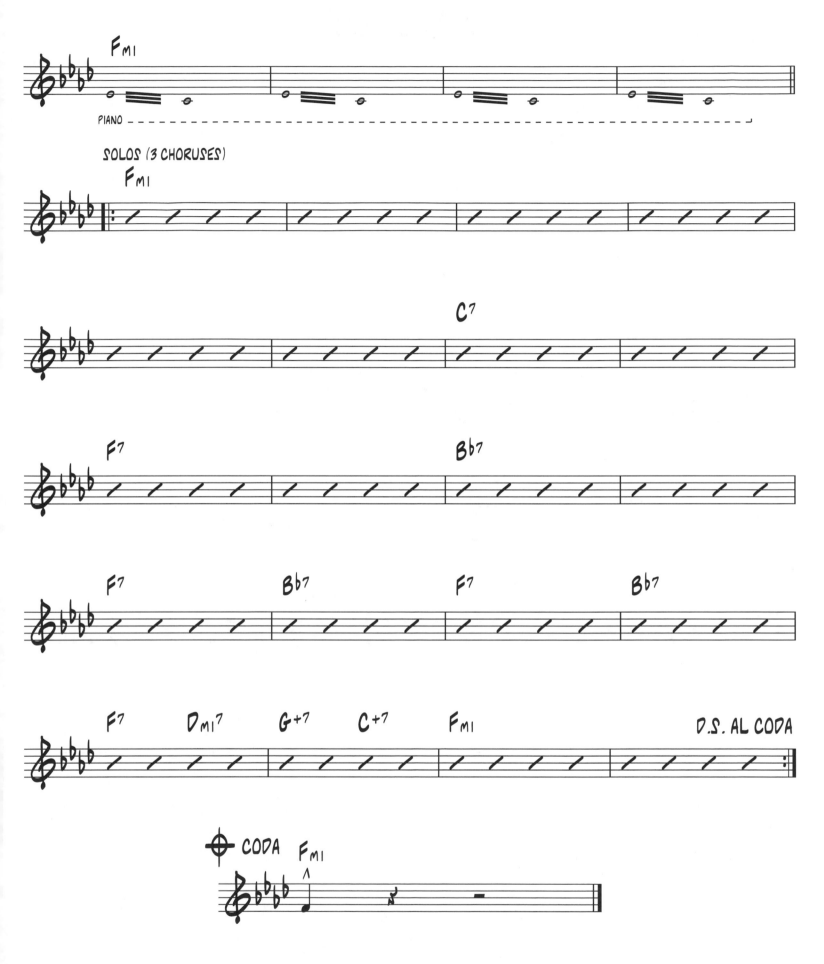

CD
◆5: SPLIT TRACK/MELODY
◆6: FULL STEREO TRACK

GARY'S NOTEBOOK

BY LEE MORGAN

C VERSION

MEDIUM JAZZ WALTZ

SOLOS (2 CHORUSES)

HOCUS-POCUS

C VERSION

BY LEE MORGAN

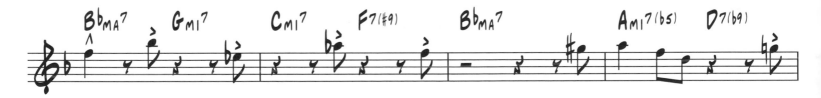

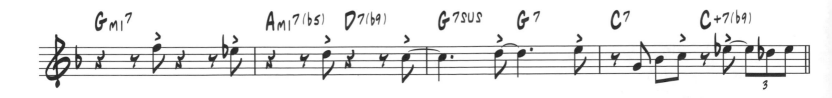

CD

◆ 9 : SPLIT TRACK/MELODY
◆ 10 : FULL STEREO TRACK

THE JOKER

BY LEE MORGAN

C VERSION

MEDIUM SWING

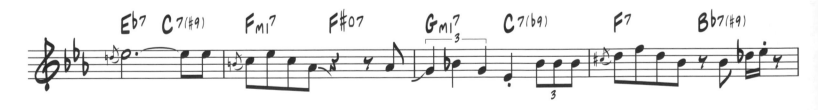

SOLOS (2 CHORUSES)

| Eb7 | C7 | Fmi7 | Bb7 | Gmi7 | C7 | Fmi7 | Bb7 |

| Bbmi7 | A7 | Ab6 | Abmi7 | Gmi7 | C7 | F7 | Bb7 |

| Eb7 | C7 | Fmi7 | Bb7 | Gmi7 | C7 | Fmi7 | Bb7 |

| Bbmi7 | A7 | Ab6 | Abmi7 | Gmi7 | C7 | Fmi7 Bb7 Eb6 |

| Bbmi7 | Eb7 | AbMA7 | |

| Cmi7 | F7 | Fmi7 | Bb7 |

| Eb7 | C7 | Fmi7 | Bb7 | Gmi7 | C7 | Fmi7 | Bb7 |

| Bbmi7 | A7 | Ab6 | Abmi7 | Gmi7 | C7 | Fmi7 Bb7 Eb6 |

D.S. AL FINE
TAKE REPEAT

LAST X ONLY

CD
⑪: SPLIT TRACK/MELODY
⑫: FULL STEREO TRACK

MR. KENYATTA

BY LEE MORGAN

C VERSION

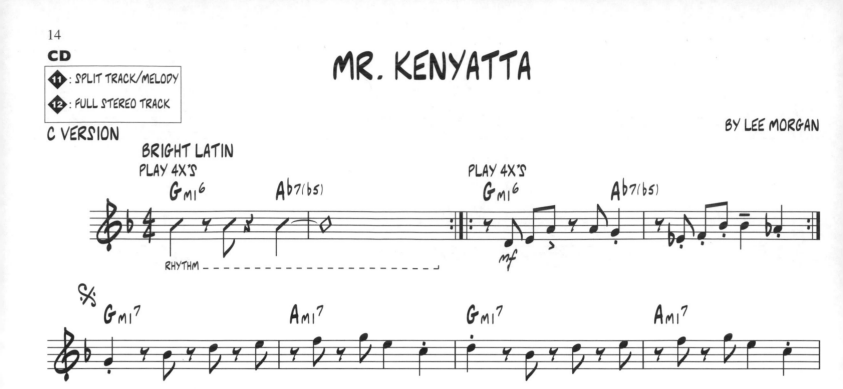

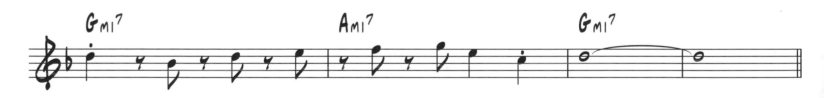

LATIN

TO CODA ⊕

SOLOS (3 CHORUSES)

SWING

LATIN

D.S. AL CODA

⊕ CODA PLAY 4X'S

MORGAN THE PIRATE

BY LEE MORGAN

C VERSION

SOLOS (2 CHORUSES)

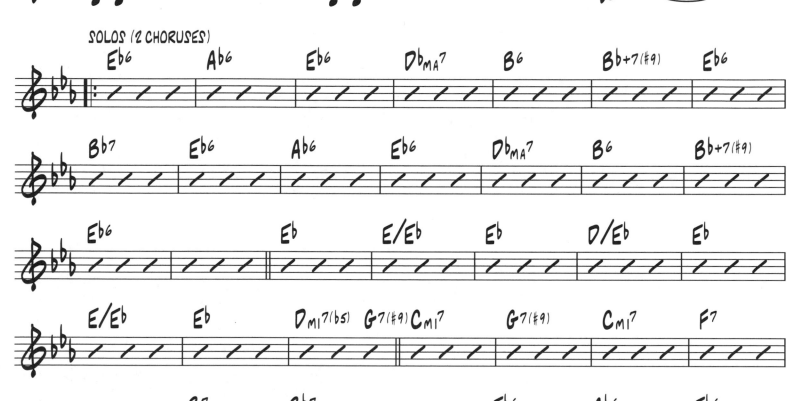

SIDEWINDER

BY LEE MORGAN

15 : SPLIT TRACK/MELODY
16 : FULL STEREO TRACK

C VERSION

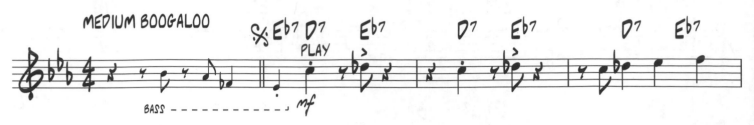

SOLOS (3 CHORUSES)

1ST X ONLY

D.S. AL CODA

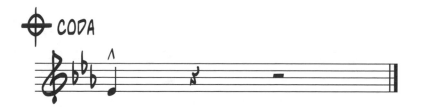

CODA

TOTEM POLE

BY LEE MORGAN

C VERSION

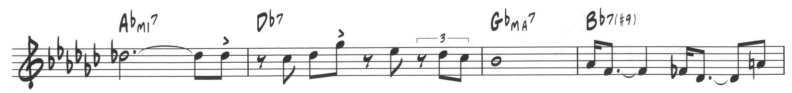

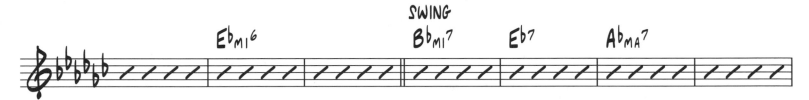

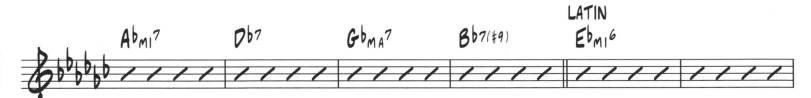

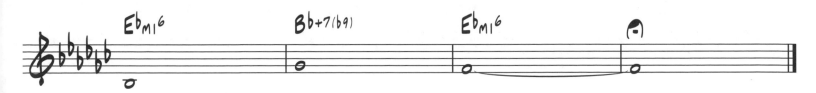

SPEEDBALL

BY LEE MORGAN

SPEEDBALL

BY LEE MORGAN

Bb VERSION

CEORA

BY LEE MORGAN

Bb VERSION

MEDIUM BOSSA

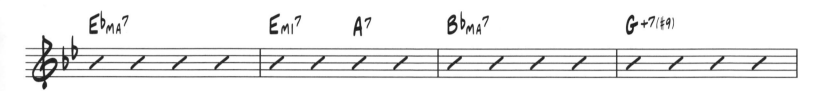

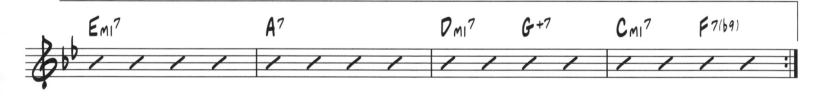

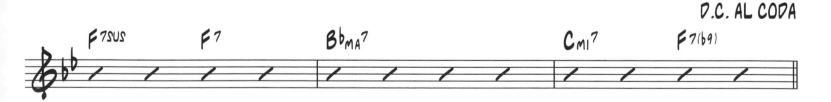

CORN BREAD

Bb VERSION

BY LEE MORGAN

MEDIUM 60'S FUNK

GARY'S NOTEBOOK

BY LEE MORGAN

Bb VERSION

MEDIUM JAZZ WALTZ

SOLOS (2 CHORUSES)

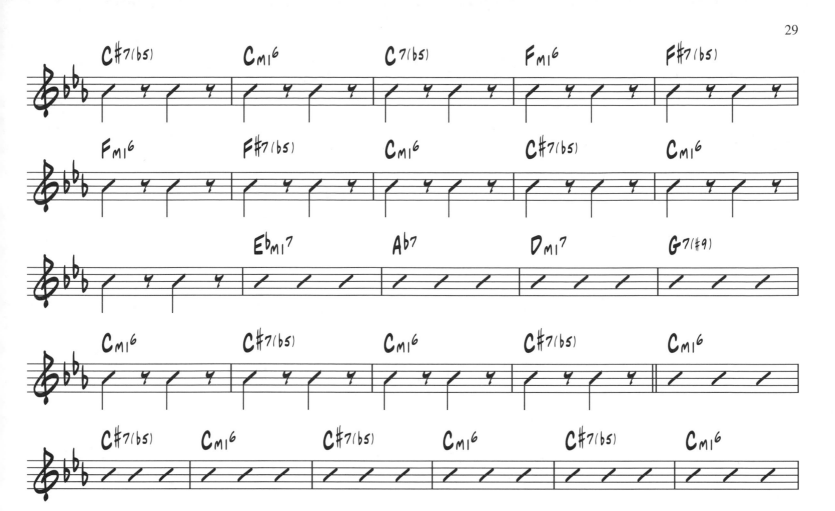

D.C. AL CODA
(TAKE 1ST REPEAT ONLY)

CD
- **7** : SPLIT TRACK/MELODY
- **8** : FULL STEREO TRACK

HOCUS-POCUS

Bb VERSION

BY LEE MORGAN

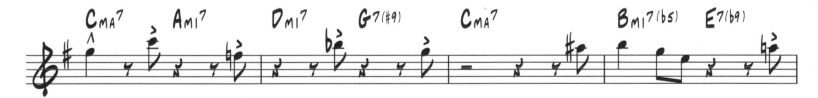

CD

◆ **9** : SPLIT TRACK/MELODY
◆ **10** : FULL STEREO TRACK

THE JOKER

BY LEE MORGAN

Bb VERSION

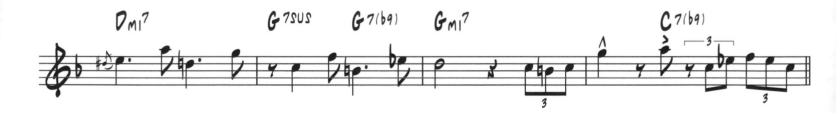

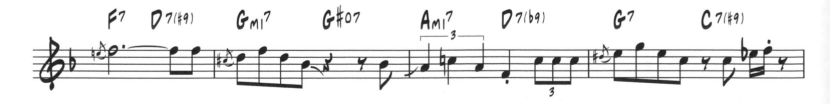

33

SOLOS (2 CHORUSES)

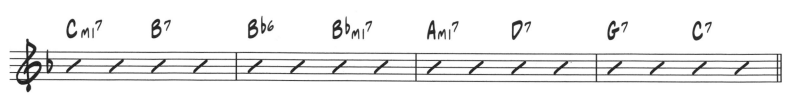

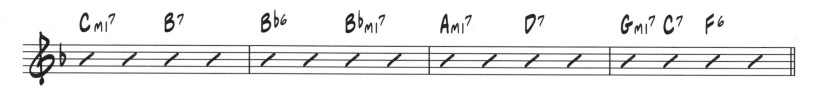

MR. KENYATTA

CD
⑪ : SPLIT TRACK/MELODY
⑫ : FULL STEREO TRACK

BY LEE MORGAN

Bb VERSION

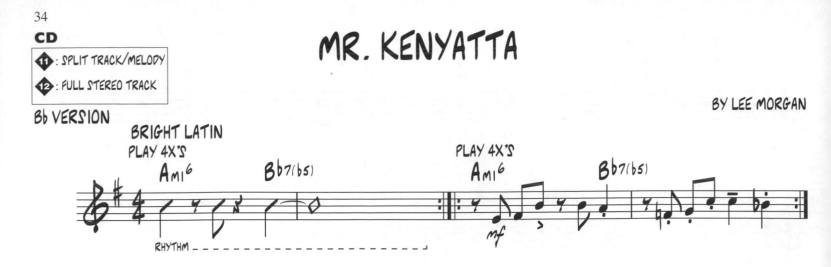

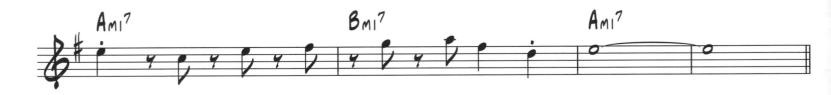

LATIN

TO CODA ⊕

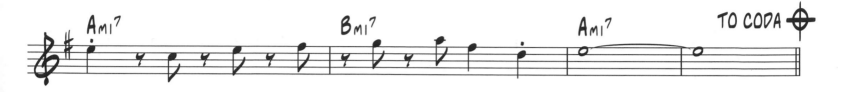

SOLOS (3 CHORUSES)

SWING

LATIN

D.S. AL CODA

⊕ CODA PLAY 4X'S

MORGAN THE PIRATE

BY LEE MORGAN

CD

⟨13⟩ : SPLIT TRACK/MELODY
⟨14⟩ : FULL STEREO TRACK

Bb VERSION

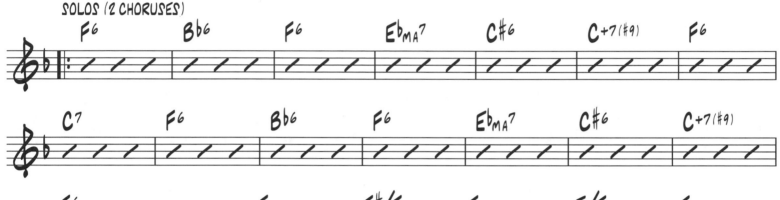

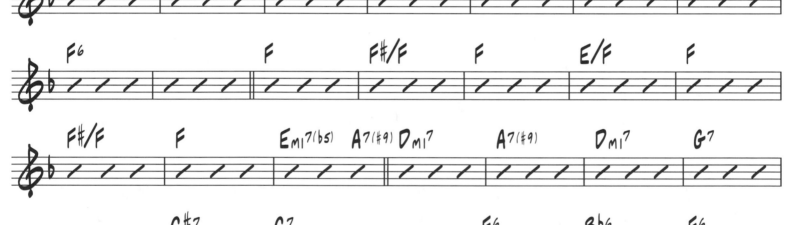

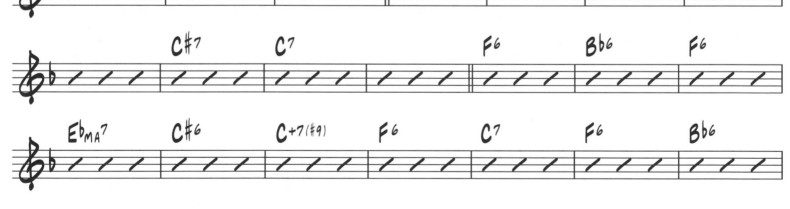

Sidewinder

BY LEE MORGAN

Bb VERSION

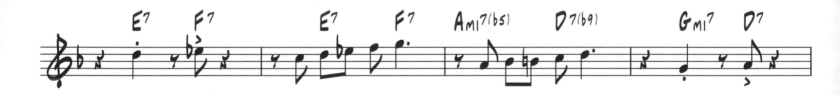

SOLOS (3 CHORUSES)

1ST X ONLY

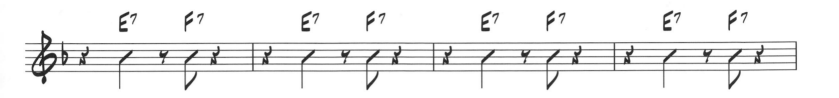

D.S. AL CODA

CODA

TOTEM POLE

BY LEE MORGAN

Bb VERSION

CEORA

BY LEE MORGAN

Eb VERSION

MEDIUM BOSSA

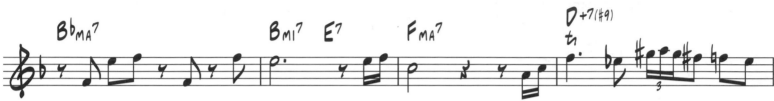

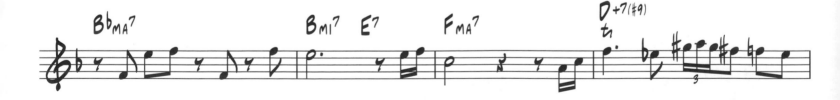

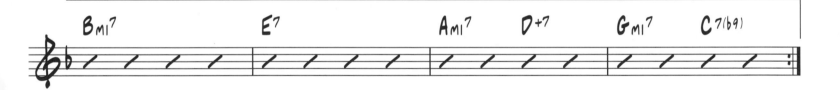

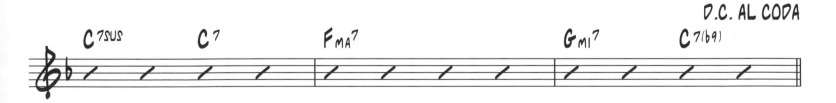

CORN BREAD

Eb VERSION

BY LEE MORGAN

MEDIUM 60'S FUNK

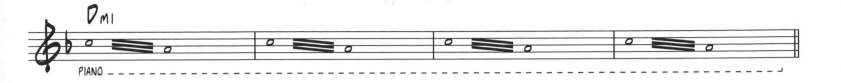

D_{MI}

PIANO -

SOLOS (3 CHORUSES)

D_{MI}

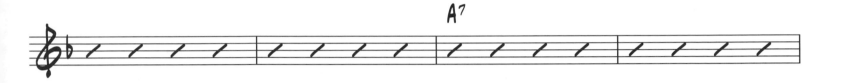

A^7

D^7 G^7

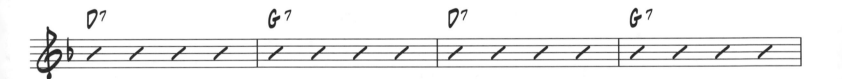

D^7 G^7 D^7 G^7

D^7 B_{MI}^7 E^{+7} A^{+7} D_{MI} D.S. AL CODA

CODA D_{MI}

CD

◆ **5** : SPLIT TRACK/MELODY
◆ **6** : FULL STEREO TRACK

GARY'S NOTEBOOK

BY LEE MORGAN

Eb VERSION

MEDIUM JAZZ WALTZ

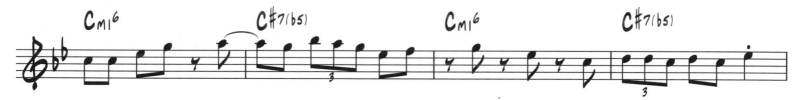

SOLOS (2 CHORUSES)

CD
7 : SPLIT TRACK/MELODY
8 : FULL STEREO TRACK

HOCUS-POCUS

Eb VERSION

BY LEE MORGAN

THE JOKER

BY LEE MORGAN

Eb VERSION

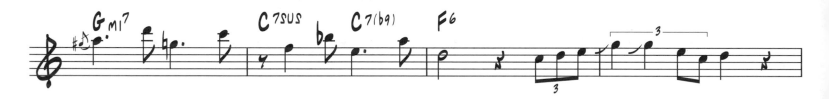

SOLOS (2 CHORUSES)

MR. KENYATTA

BY LEE MORGAN

Eb VERSION

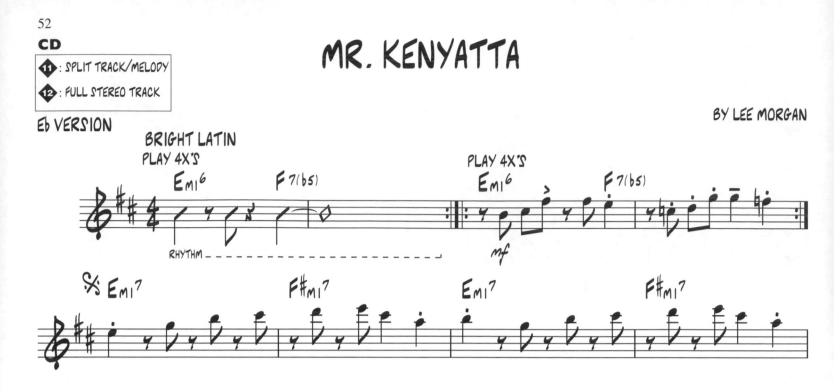

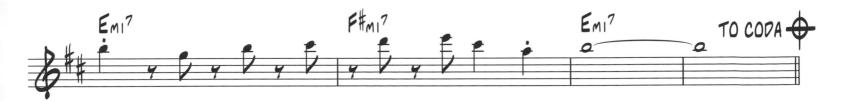

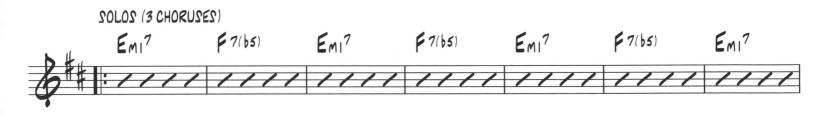

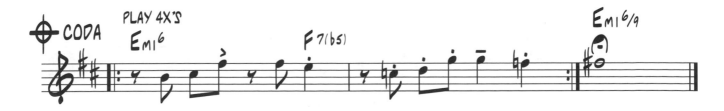

MORGAN THE PIRATE

BY LEE MORGAN

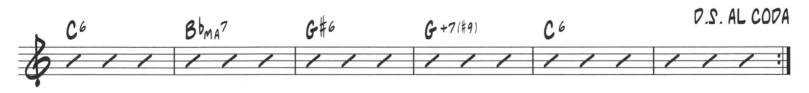

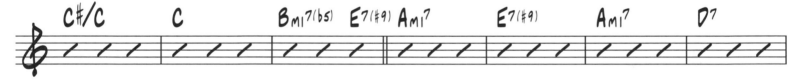

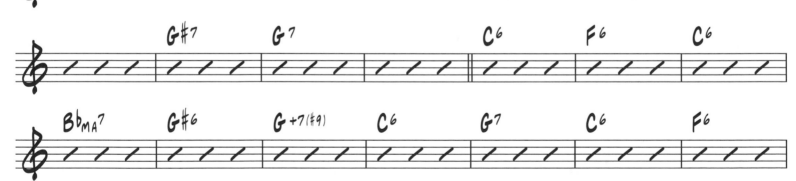

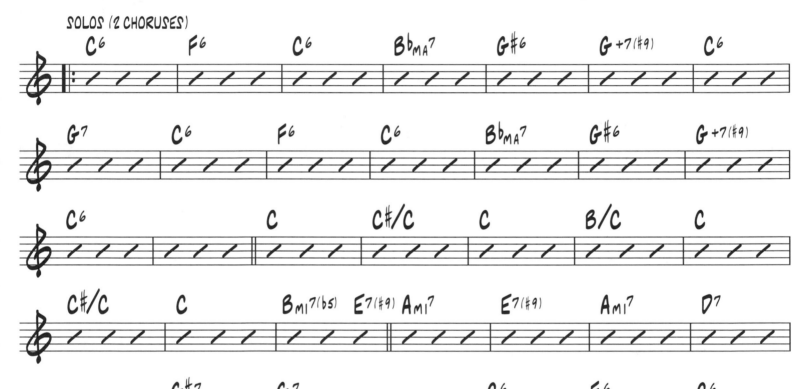

Sidewinder

BY LEE MORGAN

Eb VERSION

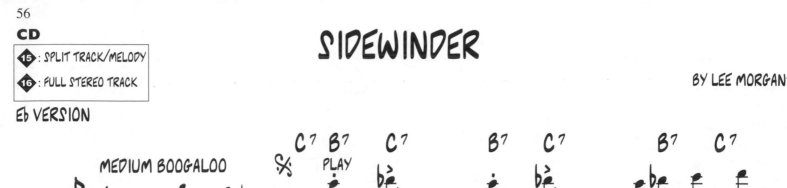

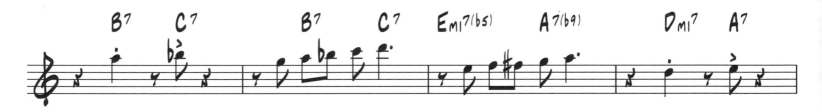

SOLOS (3 CHORUSES)

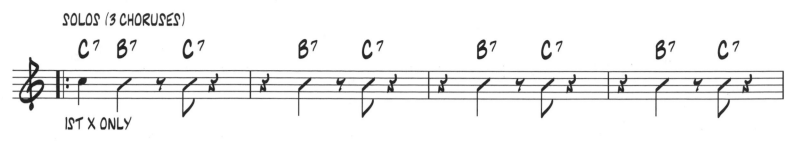

1ST X ONLY

D.S. AL CODA

CODA

TOTEM POLE

BY LEE MORGAN

Eb VERSION

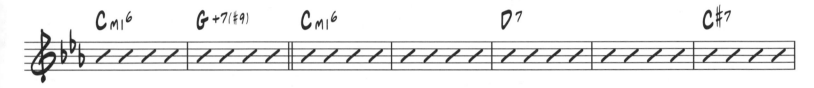

SPEEDBALL

BY LEE MORGAN

SPEEDBALL

BY LEE MORGAN

CD

1: SPLIT TRACK/MELODY
2: FULL STEREO TRACK

CEORA

BY LEE MORGAN

𝄢: C VERSION

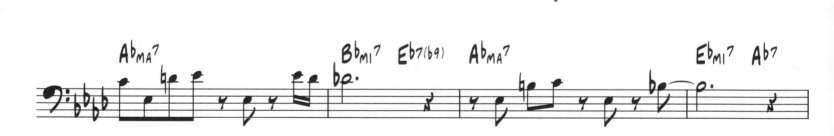

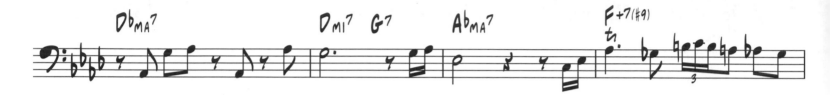

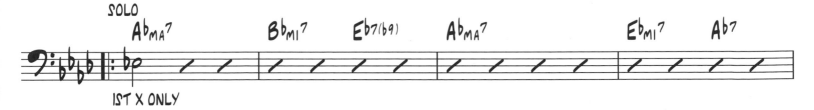

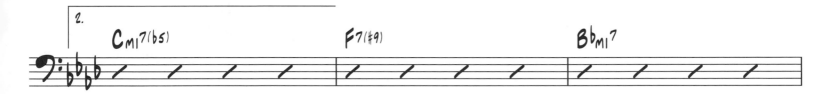

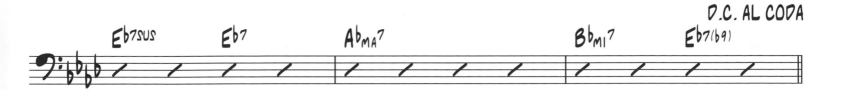

CORN BREAD

𝄢: C VERSION

BY LEE MORGAN

MEDIUM 60'S FUNK

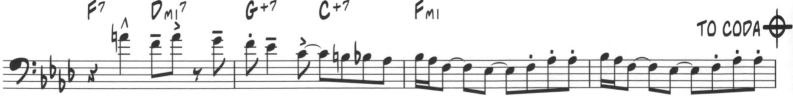

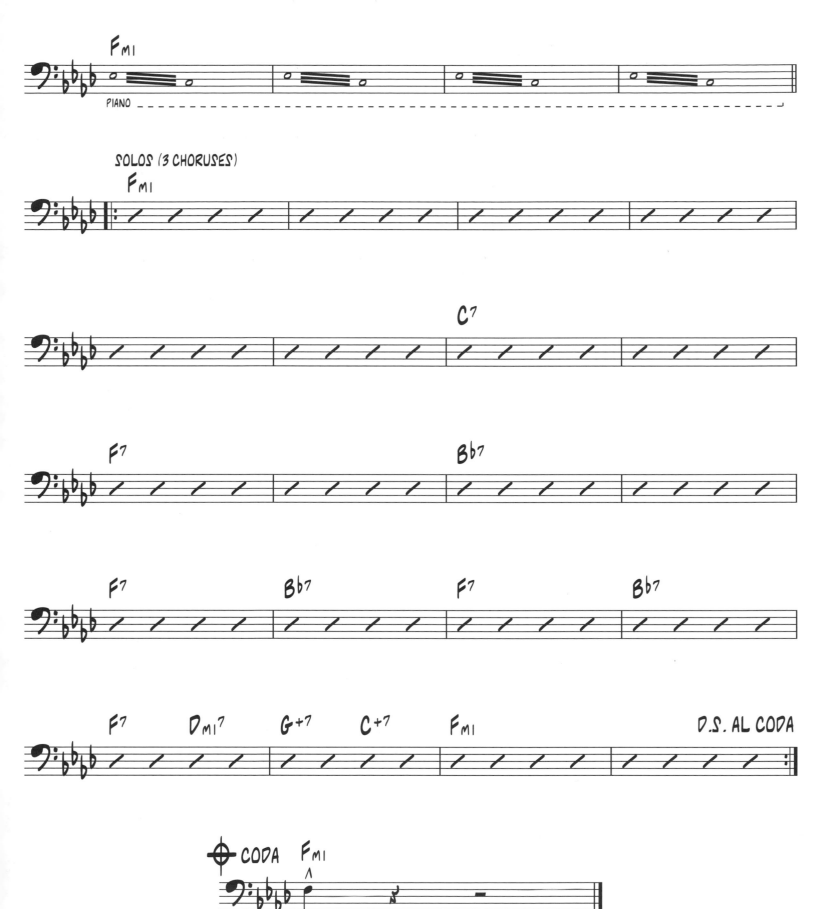

CD
⑤ : SPLIT TRACK/MELODY
⑥ : FULL STEREO TRACK

GARY'S NOTEBOOK

BY LEE MORGAN

𝄢: C VERSION

MEDIUM JAZZ WALTZ

HOCUS-POCUS

♮: C VERSION

BY LEE MORGAN

THE JOKER

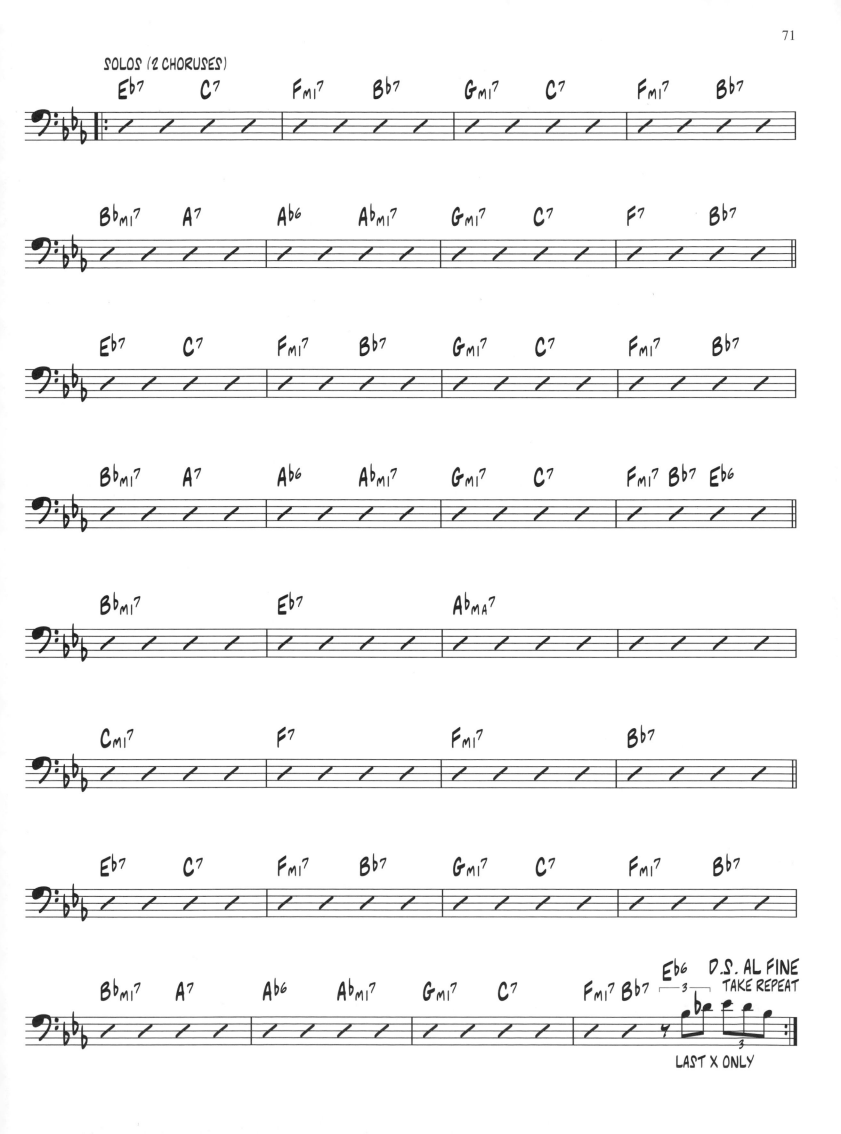

CD

MR. KENYATTA

BY LEE MORGAN

🎼: C VERSION BRIGHT LATIN

SWING

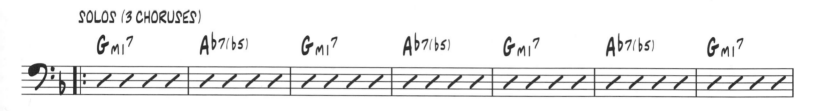

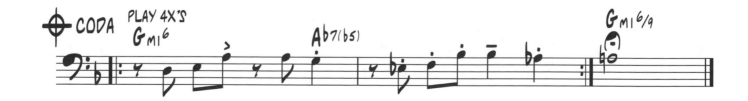

MORGAN THE PIRATE

BY LEE MORGAN

: C VERSION

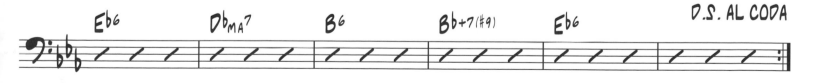

SIDEWINDER

BY LEE MORGAN

: C VERSION

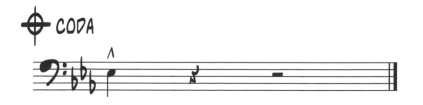

TOTEM POLE

BY LEE MORGAN

𝄢 : C VERSION

MEDIUM LATIN

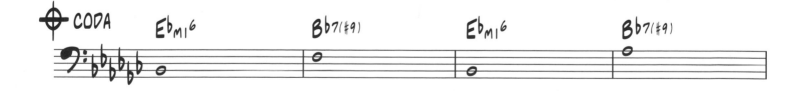

For use with all B-flat, E-flat, Bass Clef and C instruments, the Jazz Play-Along® Series is the ultimate learning tool for all jazz musicians. With musician-friendly lead sheets, melody cues, and other split-track choices on the included CD, these first-of-a-kind packages help you master improvisation while playing some of the greatest tunes of all time. FOR STUDY, each tune includes a split track with: melody cue with proper style and inflection • professional rhythm tracks • choruses for soloing • removable bass part • removable piano part. FOR PERFORMANCE, each tune also has: an additional full stereo accompaniment track (no melody) • additional choruses for soloing.

1A. MAIDEN VOYAGE/ALL BLUES
00843158 .... $15.99

1. DUKE ELLINGTON
00841644 .... $16.95

2. MILES DAVIS
00841645 .... $16.95

3. THE BLUES
00841646 .... $16.99

4. JAZZ BALLADS
00841691 .... $16.99

5. BEST OF BEBOP
00841689 .... $16.95

6. JAZZ CLASSICS WITH EASY CHANGES
00841690 .... $16.99

7. ESSENTIAL JAZZ STANDARDS
00843000 .... $16.99

8. ANTONIO CARLOS JOBIM AND THE ART OF THE BOSSA NOVA
00843001 .... $16.95

9. DIZZY GILLESPIE
00843002 .... $16.99

10. DISNEY CLASSICS
00843003 .... $16.99

11. RODGERS AND HART FAVORITES
00843004 .... $16.99

12. ESSENTIAL JAZZ CLASSICS
00843005 .... $16.99

13. JOHN COLTRANE
00843006 .... $16.95

14. IRVING BERLIN
00843007 .... $15.99

15. RODGERS & HAMMERSTEIN
00843008 .... $15.99

16. COLE PORTER
00843009 .... $15.95

17. COUNT BASIE
00843010 .... $16.95

18. HAROLD ARLEN
00843011 .... $15.95

19. COOL JAZZ
00843012 .... $15.95

20. CHRISTMAS CAROLS
00843080 .... $14.95

21. RODGERS AND HART CLASSICS
00843014 .... $14.95

22. WAYNE SHORTER
00843015 .... $16.95

23. LATIN JAZZ
00843016 .... $16.95

24. EARLY JAZZ STANDARDS
00843017 .... $14.95

25. CHRISTMAS JAZZ
00843018 .... $16.95

26. CHARLIE PARKER
00843019 .... $16.95

27. GREAT JAZZ STANDARDS
00843020 .... $16.99

28. BIG BAND ERA
00843021 .... $15.99

29. LENNON AND MCCARTNEY
00843022 .... $16.95

30. BLUES' BEST
00843023 .... $15.99

31. JAZZ IN THREE
00843024 .... $15.99

32. BEST OF SWING
00843025 .... $15.99

33. SONNY ROLLINS
00843029 .... $15.95

34. ALL TIME STANDARDS
00843030 .... $15.99

35. BLUESY JAZZ
00843031 .... $16.99

36. HORACE SILVER
00843032 .... $16.99

37. BILL EVANS
00843033 .... $16.95

38. YULETIDE JAZZ
00843034 .... $16.95

39. "ALL THE THINGS YOU ARE" & MORE JEROME KERN SONGS
00843035 .... $15.99

40. BOSSA NOVA
00843036 .... $16.99

41. CLASSIC DUKE ELLINGTON
00843037 .... $16.99

42. GERRY MULLIGAN FAVORITES
00843038 .... $16.99

43. GERRY MULLIGAN CLASSICS
00843039 .... $16.99

44. OLIVER NELSON
00843040 .... $16.95

46. BROADWAY JAZZ STANDARDS
00843042 .... $15.99

47. CLASSIC JAZZ BALLADS
00843043 .... $15.99

48. BEBOP CLASSICS
00843044 .... $16.99

49. MILES DAVIS STANDARDS
00843045 .... $16.95

50. GREAT JAZZ CLASSICS
00843046 .... $15.99

51. UP-TEMPO JAZZ
00843047 .... $15.99

52. STEVIE WONDER
00843048 .... $16.99

53. RHYTHM CHANGES
00843049 .... $15.99

54. "MOONLIGHT IN VERMONT" AND OTHER GREAT STANDARDS
00843050 .... $15.99

55. BENNY GOLSON
00843052 .... $15.95

56. "GEORGIA ON MY MIND" & OTHER SONGS BY HOAGY CARMICHAEL
00843056 .... $15.99

57. VINCE GUARALDI
00843057 .... $16.99

58. MORE LENNON AND MCCARTNEY
00843059 .... $16.99

59. SOUL JAZZ
00843060 .... $16.99

60. DEXTER GORDON
00843061 .... $15.95

61. MONGO SANTAMARIA
00843062 .... $15.95

62. JAZZ-ROCK FUSION
00843063 .... $16.99

63. CLASSICAL JAZZ
00843064 .... $14.95

64. TV TUNES
00843065 .... $14.95

65. SMOOTH JAZZ
00843066 .... $16.99